Essays of an American Citizen

By

Daniel C Symonds

Order this book online at www.trafford.com
or email orders@trafford.com

Most Trafford titles are also available at major online book retailers.

Printed in the United States of America.

ISBN: 978-1-4269-8947-6 (sc)
ISBN: 978-1-4269-8948-3 (e)

Trafford rev. 08/10/2011

 www.trafford.com

North America & international
toll-free: 1 888 232 4444 (USA & Canada)
phone: 250 383 6864 ♦ fax: 812 355 4082

Dedication

These essays are dedicated to my Mother, who encouraged me and gave me the confidence that I could achieve anything; and my Wife, who through her love and mothering of our children gave me the purpose and desire to achieve.

These essays were written for my children, my children's children and all of my family and friends.

Table of Contents

Dedication v

1. In the beginning. 1

2. The Building Blocks of Our Country 5

3. Religion & Freedom of Speech 11

4. Right of Privacy 17

5. Civil Rights 19

6. Political Parties 23

7. Elections 27

8. Congress, The Land of Special Interest and the Home of Hypocrisy 31

9. Why We Went to War with Iraq 37

10. Our Uninformed Citizenry 41

11. E-Mail Misinformation 45

12. Women in Power 51

13. Balancing the Budget 53

14. Health Care 59

15. Education 61

16. Socialism 65

Acknowledgement 67

"All that is necessary for evil to triumph is that good men do nothing." **Edmund Burke.**

1. In the beginning...

Thanks to God that he gave me stubbornness when I know I am right.
John Adams

In the late 1950's, unbeknownst to me, Congress debated a bill to raise federal employee pay. The bill passed, however, President Eisenhower vetoed it. Congress, with great assistance from the Senate's Majority Leader, Lyndon Johnson, over road the veto. My Father, a letter carrier, received his raise. I remember how happy my parents were. Looking back on that moment, it became clear to me the effect government action has on a person's life.

By the time I graduated from high school in 1968, I had a growing interest in political issues. That should come as no surprise since so much happened in that year. Martin Luther King and Robert Kennedy were assassinated, cities were burning from racial riots, and the Democratic Convention in Chicago became a centerpiece of discontent of the country's youth due to the unpopularity of the Viet Nam War.

My parent's generation was dumbfounded by the unruly behavior of the "hippies" protesting on college campuses with their long hair and slogans of "Free Love". This personally hit home on only one issue—hair length. My father and I did not get along when hair became an issue. I think my father didn't want his buddies to know that his kid had long hair and therefore, by association, had to be one of those long hair hippie commies! The older generation just didn't get it. It wasn't about hair. It was about freedom of expression.

Some of the best times I had while in college were at family holiday reunions when I would sit down with my uncles in the living room to discuss current events. Most of them were very conservative to the point where they were absolutely convinced that the communists were going to take over the world and the hippies were helping their cause by causing chaos.

Of course, I did nothing to change their fears, and I had fun making outrageous comments just to get their reactions. Some of it was instigated by my Uncle Fred. He did seem to get a kick out of me debating the issues with my other uncles. Even though he was my oldest uncle, he probably was the most moderate. I had another uncle who was incredibly naïve and gullible. He once said he heard that all students at Indiana University smoked pot. In order to get a reaction from all, I told him that was absolutely true even though it wasn't close to being true.

The next big political event was Watergate. What fun. Most of my generation believed Nixon was guilty as sin, and as expected, my parents generation thought the charges were trumped up by the liberal *Washington Post* and *CBS News*. Woodward and Bernstein of the Post and Dan Rather of CBS were heroes to the young and were most certainly thought of as "communist sympathizers" by our parents.

When the Watergate hearings started, all my friends and I watched as history was being made virtually every day. When Alexander Butterfield told the committee that Nixon taped all of his conversations in the Oval Office, it was obvious that all Nixon had to do to clear his name was to voluntarily give up the tapes of his conversations in question. He wouldn't. His guilt was never in question after that.

My father told me when I was in my teens, he didn't care if I was a Democrat or Republican. The important thing was to know why. I'm a moderate on fiscal matters. I believe both parties have some good ideas about how to run this country and how to pay for it. I'm a liberal on social issues. Let the people do whatever they want as long as it does not interfere with anyone else's rights.

More times than not, I vote Democratic and in fact I am registered as such. I have voted many times, especially in the 70's and 80's, for moderate Republicans. Unfortunately, they have become almost extinct today.

What follows is an expression of my opinions in essay form. The opinions are based upon FACTS. The facts are uncontestable. My opinions are also based upon over sixty years of living, observing, reading and discussing political issues. Perhaps the most important source of my opinions is experiences I have had during my life and what impressions those experiences have left on me.

It is not my intention to get you to agree with every opinion I hold, although you should. My intention is to get you to think about these issues on your own. Listen to others and read about the issues, but don't be overly influenced by what one person or one article says unless there is factual support for that position. Many people who mouth off are either ignorant or have their own agenda. Think it out for yourself. Question authority. If you read or hear something that doesn't appear truthful, it probably isn't.

Research the statement to determine its veracity. What is important is to be able to give an opinion and support your opinion with documented facts --not upon innuendo, prejudices, biases or hearsay. Know what you are talking about. Be able to defend your position, and don't back down when you know you are right.

2. The Building Blocks of Our Country

In framing a government, which is to be administered by men over men, the great difficulty lies in this: you must first enable the government to control the governed, and in the next place, oblige it to control itself. James Madison

A recent Rasmussen Poll published on November 23, 2010, indicated that 39% of likely US voters believe the government is currently operating within the limits of the constitution, 44% disagree and 17% aren't sure. How many of these voters have ever read the constitution or could in 25 words or less describe what the constitution is? Sure, some could, but the most honest people in this survey are probably the 17% who said they weren't sure.

Let's face it. People for the most part, have no idea what the Constitution and more specifically the Bill of Rights says or stands for. For that matter they probably don't even know the form of our government.

Newsweek recently asked 1000 United States citizens to take America's official citizenship test-- the test that foreigners take to become citizens of our country. The master test consists of 100 questions covering American government, systems of government, rights and responsibilities, American history and integrated civics. Of those questions, ten are given in each test and in order to pass the test, six must be answered correctly.

Thirty-eight percent of those tested, all being United States citizens, flunked it. *Newsweek, How Dumb Are We?* March 28, 2011. Twenty-nine percent could not name the Vice-President. Forty-four percent could not define the Bill of Rights and six percent couldn't even circle the date of Independence Day on a calendar!!! Two thirds of those tested could not identify our country's economic system as capitalism. You think that is bad? Nine percent of those tested could not name the ocean on the west coast of the United States.

My all time favorite however, is this one—65% of those tested could not say what happened at the Constitutional Convention. Seriously, what do these people think happened? Do you think they could answer what happens at a baseball game? They play baseball. So using our great powers of reasoning, I would have thought that most people would have known or guessed that what happened at the Constitutional Convention was the delegates wrote the Constitution.

Our Form of Government

Democracy is defined in part as Government by the people, exercised either directly or through elected representatives; a political or social unit that has such a government where majority rules. *Houghton Mifflin* dictionary. The dictionary defines a federal republic as a form of government made up of a federal state with a constitution and self-governing subunits. *www. dictionary.reference.com* Most people would say our form of government is a democracy, however, the United States is really a federal republic.

The Constitution

The Constitution is an outline as to the formation of the federal government, which branch has what powers and what powers the government has over its citizens. It starts with a preamble which basically says, "We the People" establish this Constitution in order to get our act together, although not exactly in those terms.

Article I establishes the legislative body of our country--Congress. It divides the body into two houses, advises the requirements for being a member of each body, the term length of service and the powers each house has.

Article II sets forth the executive branch which is lead by the President, with second in command being the Vice-President. This article gives the minimum qualifications for being the President, the term length of office and states how the President and Vice-President shall be elected. The article also defines the executive powers of the President, sets the grounds for impeachment of the President and requires the President to periodically advise Congress as to the state of the union.

Article III establishes the judiciary branch and advises as to the subject matter jurisdiction of the federal courts. Article IV gives "full faith and credit" to all laws of the individual states and indicates that the citizens of each state shall have the same "privileges and immunities" of citizens of every other state. The article also gives Congress the power to admit other states and guarantees to those states a republican form of government and protection from invasion and against domestic violence.

Article V sets forth the procedure for amending the constitution. Article VI states that all contracts entered into before the ratification of the constitution are valid against the United States; the Constitution, all federal laws and treaties shall be the law of the land; and all federal officials shall be bound by oath or affirmation to support the constitution. Article VII advises when ratification of the constitution takes place.

The Bill of Rights

A Bill of Rights is what the people are entitled to against every government, and what no just government should refuse, or rest on inference. Thomas Jefferson

In the late 1780's many states questioned whether they should ratify the Constitution without articles dealing with individual and state rights. Some states made a request for a bill of rights. These requests led to the authorship of same.

This document, the first ten amendments to the Constitution, is the backbone of our individual freedoms. The First Amendment guarantees the right to free speech, free press, free assembly and the freedom to freely worship any religion or no religion at all. It also allows its citizens to petition the government for redress of grievances.

The Second Amendment gives the citizens the right to bear arms. The Third Amendment is probably not relevant at all today. It states that no soldier shall be quartered in anyone's home without the owner's permission in a manner to be prescribed by law.

The Fourth Amendment prohibits unreasonable searches and seizures and states that a warrant can only be issued based upon probable cause and must be specific as to the place to be searched and the things to be seized.

The Fifth Amendment states that no person shall have to answer to a capital or infamous crime unless on a presentment or indictment issued by a Grand Jury. The amendment also prohibits double jeopardy and self incrimination in a criminal matter. In addition it states a person cannot be deprived of life, liberty or property without due process of the law. Private property cannot be taken for public use without just compensation.

The Sixth Amendment guarantees a speedy and public trial by an impartial jury in criminal matters in the jurisdiction where the crime was committed. The accused must be advised of the charges, be allowed to confront his accusers and call his own witnesses and have counsel for his defense.

The Seventh Amendment guarantees trial by jury of civil matters wherein the value of the controversy is in excess of twenty dollars. The Eighth Amendment prohibits excessive bail, excessive fines or cruel and unusual punishment be inflicted.

The Ninth Amendment states that the enumeration of rights in the Constitution shall not be construed to deny or disparage other rights retained by the people. The Tenth Amendment indicates that the powers not delegated to the United States or prohibited by it to the states are reserved for the states or to the people.

It would be interesting to have our citizens respond to a survey asking them whether they would agree or disagree with statements in the Bill of Rights. Of course they would not be advised that the statements are part of the document.

How would the public respond to questions like, "Should our citizens have the right to own firearms?" or "Should the United States be barred from declaring Christianity as the country's acknowledged religion?" I'll bet the results would be very interesting, and we would be surprised to find that a fair amount of our citizens disagree with some of the individual rights we currently have.

American Civil Liberties Union

For the record: yes, I am a card-carrying member of the ACLU. But the more important question is why aren't you…? Now, this is an organization whose sole purpose is to defend the Bill of Rights, so it naturally begs the question: Why would a senator, his party's most powerful spokesman and a candidate for President, choose to reject upholding the Constitution? An American President, President Andrew Shepard defending his membership in the ACLU and inquiring why his political adversary is not.

This organization is the most misunderstood entity in our country. The general feeling is that the ACLU spends its time defending crazy people and their particular misguided ideas. This is true if we believe that anyone who disagrees with the norm is crazy or misguided.

If you are an American citizen, 40 year old straight white Christian male, without a criminal record, you probably will never need the services of the ACLU. Why? Because as a general rule, no one would have strong feelings against what you obviously stand for. Your rights are already protected simply because there is nothing about you that people would vehemently oppose. How difficult would it be for you to obtain a permit from the city to organize a Patriot Day parade on Main Street? Pretty easy.

But what if you are an American citizen and a gay black female Muslim who wants a permit to be able to organize a pro-Nazi march in a Jewish neighborhood? You may need the ACLU to help you get that permit. Why? Because your beliefs clearly do not conform to the norm in our society. Many citizens would be violently opposed to you and your beliefs for many reasons. They may hate gays, blacks, Muslims, or Nazis. They may oppose everything that you stand for and truly believe that you are the anti-Christ. Negative public pressure might weigh so heavy as to force officials to deny you the permit. What do you do? You call the ACLU.

It is important to note, however, that the white male and the black female have exactly the same rights and freedoms guaranteed to them under the Bill of Rights. Thus, the need for the ACLU.

Patriotism

Patriotism is more than just a bumper sticker on the back of your car, or putting a hand over your heart during the playing of the national anthem. Neither political party has a monopoly on patriotism although you might think otherwise at times.

Some citizens believe that if you don't agree with the governments' positions on issues of great importance, you are unpatriotic! If you disagree with the status quo, you don't love your country. How pathetic is that?

To me patriotism is always loving your country but not always agreeing with its leaders. Patriotism is supporting our troops but protesting the war. It is defending the Bill of Rights no matter how unpopular the subject matter is.

Patriotism is peaceful protest. It is respecting every citizens' rights regardless of whether you agree with them or not.

3. Religion & Freedom of Speech

Congress shall make no law respecting an establishment of religion, or prohibiting the free exercise thereof; The Establishment and Free Exercise clauses of the First Amendment to our Constitution

Most people in our country have never read those words. In fact, if you read it to them, they probably wouldn't know the source or what it means. It is part of the first amendment to our Constitution, the first Bill of our rights.

To me the wording is clear and unambiguous. The government cannot force you to believe or stop you from believing. It cannot make you pray or stop you from praying. It cannot make you believe in God or stop you from believing in God. The government cannot "establish" a religion or interfere with the "free exercise" of your religion.

Separation of Church and State is imperative in our free society. For some reason people have a very tough time respecting this principle of our law. Our country was found upon a foundation of religious freedom. Yet some of our citizens seem to think that religious freedom is fine as long as you agree with them—as long as you believe that this country is a "Christian" country. "God" help you if you don't!

The first amendment, however, clearly states that the government is prohibited from establishing religion—any religion, Christian or otherwise!

Why are we so arrogant to think that this is a Christian country? This is a country, period. Our citizens worship many different religions and some of our citizens do not worship at all. The United States is no more a Christian country than it is a white person's country or a country of brunettes.

Furthermore, God does not love the United States of America! God is not on our side either! You want to know why? God doesn't love entities or governments. God doesn't love the Red Cross or Apple or General Motors either. God loves Americans! He loves Americans and he loves Germans and Chinese and every other person on this Earth. He is on everyone's side!

Apparently there are some in this country who are not big fans of the first amendment separation of church and state. Here's a quote from the late Rev. Jerry Falwell, "The idea that religion and politics don't mix was invented by the Devil to keep Christians from running their own country." Those so called devils have names--James Madison, Thomas Jefferson and George Mason who were, for the most part, the authors of the Bill of Rights.

Establishing Religion

Public schools are financed by taxpayer money. Some of our citizens believe that creationism should be taught in our public schools. This is a plain and simple example of the government establishing religion. This is a clear violation of the separation of church and state. Further, teaching creationism in public schools is about as likely as teaching evolution in our churches. Do you think we will ever see that? I doubt it.

Some people have a hard time with the prayer issue as well. They say, anyone should be allowed to pray in a public school. Guess what? Anyone can. There is no law and I guarantee you that there will never be a law that prohibits a person from praying anywhere in this country. Students do it every day, usually right before taking a test. The only limitation is that a public school cannot organize students to pray or for any other religious purpose.

Prohibiting the Free Exercise of Religion

As I write this, rumors are flying all over about a mosque being built at "Ground Zero" in New York at the site of the terrorist attacks on September 11, 2001. This of course is untrue. As usual, ignorance prevails by the masses.

The mosque is in a building which was actually partly destroyed in the attacks of 9-11. The mosque has been used for prayers by Muslims for some time, and no one has had any problem with it. Now, the members of the mosque want to build a community center within the building. People are in an uproar, not because a center is being built but because Muslims have a mosque there at "Ground Zero" and the terrorists were Muslims.

The government cannot do anything about this because of the free exercise clause, but, of course, some of our citizens want it stopped. Clearly, these people are interfering with Muslims freely exercising their right to worship as they see fit.

By the way, the mosque isn't at Ground Zero. It's two blocks away.

Here's a "what if" for you. What if Catholics in an Italian neighborhood want to build a church. Citizens protest the building of the Catholic church because the Mafia is a criminal organization and its members consist mostly of Italians. What do you think about that? Isn't that what we are saying to the Muslims in New York? Offended yet? Maybe not if you're not Italian or Muslim, and that's the problem.

Organized Religion

I admit I have a problem with organized religion. I believe in God as the creator of the Universe, but I question man's interpretation of him. My cousin, Beth, said it best to me a few years ago, "God created us in his image. Organized religion creates God in its image." She hit it right on the head.

Every religion has its own idea of how God should be represented or interpreted. Each one determines an acceptable code for its members—

that which its members should or should not do. How about this? God created us in his image, whatever that image was. He loves us all equally and unconditionally and he favors no country, religion, race or individual.

I also believe in evolution. Believing in God and accepting evolution is not a contrary opinion. Maybe evolution was part of God's plan. A *Gallup Poll* in 2008 found that 44% of Americans believe that God created humans in their present form within the last 10,000 years. I would suggest to you that those 44% also probably believe that the Universe is 10,000 years old even though the scientific evidence of the universe's age in years is well into the billions.

As noted above, each religion has its own code of right and wrong. Of course, every religion has some commonality—don't kill, don't steal… unless it's in the name of God! But then there are some religious leaders who tell their congregations the most hateful things that one could imagine. Here's my favorite from Falwell, "AIDS is not just God's punishment for homosexuals; it is God's punishment for the society that tolerates homosexuals". Another example of hateful rhetoric in the name of God is noted below from Reverend Fred Phelps of the *Westboro Baptist Church.*

I have also noticed that so called Christians are more likely to judge other people rather than just minding their own business and letting others live the lives that they have chosen. These religious zealots believe everything in the Bible is absolutely true, and only those who believe that Jesus Christ is his or her savior will go to heaven. So, presumably every other person who has a different religion or who is agnostic or atheist or never even heard of Jesus Christ is going to hell. It should be quite a crowded place.

I think Norman Mailer had it right when he said, "If God is all good, then He is not all powerful. If God is all powerful then He is not all good." His point was that if God was all good and all powerful he would not have allowed the unspeakable crimes and wars that have occurred to humanity over the millenniums. He would not let the young die of disease or allow people to die of starvation.

So what is the deal? Is God all good and all loving? Does He choose not to control or direct the lives of mere mortals but instead gives us everlasting life after we leave our mortal binds? Or is He all powerful with the ability to choose our fate no matter the suffering? Or is He both? I hope He is all loving for all of our sakes.

Freedom of Speech

You want free speech? Let's see you acknowledge a man whose words make your blood boil, who's standing center stage advocating at the top of his lungs that which you would spend a life time opposing at the top of yours… Show me that, defend that, celebrate that in your classrooms. Then, you can stand up and sing about the "land of the free". An American President

So how far does "freedom of speech" stretch in this country? A very long way. Just to show you how far, I give you the Westboro Baptist Church of Topeka, Kansas.

Reverend Fred Phelps and his congregation, which apparently is mostly his family, protest at military funerals throughout the country to draw attention to their belief that US military casualties in Iraq and Afghanistan are God's punishment for the country's tolerance towards homosexuality.

I'm not making this up! They wave posters near soldier funerals that say, "THANK GOD FOR DEAD SOLDIERS", "GOD HATES FAGS" and "PRAY FOR MORE DEAD SOLDIERS".

Albert Snyder, whose military son Matthew was killed in Iraq, sued the church for intentional infliction of emotional distress for protesting during his son's funeral. Westboro's protest was done while complying with local guidance and did not interfere or disrupt the funeral as the protest was done quietly 1000 feet from the funeral site. Snyder won a verdict of five million dollars at the trial level. The Court of Appeals reversed.

The United States Supreme Court agreed to hear the case and voted 8-1 to affirm the Court of Appeals decision to vacate the trial court verdict. Chief Justice John Roberts wrote the opinion of the court and stated in part:

Speech is powerful. It can stir people to action, move them to tears of both joy and sorrow, and - as it did here - inflict great pain. On the facts before us, we cannot react to that pain by punishing the speaker. As a Nation we have chosen a different course - to protect even hurtful speech on public issues to ensure that we do not stifle public debate. That choice requires that we shield Westboro from tort liability for its picketing in this case.

The Supreme Court's decision was correct. I know the Rev and his congregational members are ignorant bigots, but freedom of speech allows ignorant bigots to speak just like the rest of us. That is part of the cost of living in a free society. Freedom of speech is not only a right for those citizens who make statements people like to hear. It goes much deeper than that. Just ask Reverend Phelps.

4. Right of Privacy

Tolerance implies no lack of commitment to one's own beliefs. Rather it condemns the oppression or persecution of others. John F Kennedy

In 1965 the United States Supreme Court determined that the citizens of this country had a right to privacy. The case was *Griswold v Connecticut*. The Court struck down a state law prohibiting the possession, sale and distribution of contraceptives to married couples. The Court's opinion indicated that there was a body of rights or guarantees implied in the Constitution which created a "zone of privacy".

This "right of privacy" has been expanded as issues have arisen in years since *Griswold*, including the right of a patient to terminate life extending medical treatment; the right of a person to possess and view pornography; and of course, the hot button issue of abortion.

No one should have to worry about lawful interference while reading books, looking at photographs or watching movies or television which some may think are obscene or inappropriate. This is not to say that the production or distribution of some things extend the right of privacy.

As an example think of viewing pictures of people who have been murdered. Certainly murder is illegal but looking at a photo of someone who has been murdered should not be illegal no matter how sick some may think viewing such photos is. Individuals should be allowed to view any reproduction of an event even if the event is illegal.

Abortion

Abortion is legal, but with certain restrictions as medical technology improves. This issue is such a hot bed of controversy that people on many occasions cannot think clearly because of the emotional baggage.

Those who oppose abortions basically take two positions, one legal and one of faith. The legal argument and one that has been brought forth since the <u>Roe v Wade</u> decision was issued in 1973 is that the right of privacy is not a constitutional guarantee and therefore cannot be extended to a woman's right to choose. The faith based issue is that life begins at conception.

The latter issue brings many questions to mind. I personally cannot argue with anyone concerning their belief that life begins at conception. I don't believe it, but I can't prove it doesn't. I do know this. A fetus cannot survive outside the womb until a certain time period elapses. Therefore, my belief, being pro-choice, is that abortion should be legal until it's medically possible for the fetus to survive, with or without medical assistance.

If pro-lifers believe that abortion is murder, do they believe that women should be prosecuted for having abortions? If a woman does not follow her Doctor's pre-natal instructions or receives no pre-natal attention from a Doctor, and the fetus is delivered stillborn or miscarried, should the woman be prosecuted for negligent homicide or even voluntary manslaughter? How about if you follow all instructions, but have a miscarriage. Should you be prosecuted for involuntary manslaughter? What if you are pregnant and you smoke or abuse alcohol or take street drugs and something is physically or mentally wrong with your baby. Should you be criminally prosecuted?

Also, if abortion is murder, it must always be murder. So any pregnancy due to rape or incest must be allowed to proceed to a live birth. No exceptions. Anything else would be inconsistent with the pro-life belief.

5. Civil Rights

Civil Rights opened the windows. When you open the windows, it does not mean that everybody will get through. We must create our own opportunities. Mary Frances Berry, former Chairperson of the Civil Rights Commission

Civil Rights legislation was necessary in our country due to the discrimination and unequal treatment of certain groups in our society. These groups to various degrees were being discriminated in employment, housing and in access to public accommodations. The law corrected the inequality, however, it didn't change individual beliefs, bias or discriminatory behavior. That takes time, and society is still dealing with changes in our thinking process.

Most people still have some bias and/or discriminatory beliefs. Their beliefs may not dominate their lives like it does in hate groups, but it always is there just below the surface. Society today requires all people to come in contact with others of different race, religion, gender and sexual preference. For the most part, people handle this in a civilized manner, but that doesn't mean they like it.

People are still stereotyped. Examples of this are numerous. A man (woman) is driving down the road and a woman (man) cuts him (her) off. The normal response is , "Did you see what that bitch (ass hole) just did?" Clearly woman translates to bitch and man translates to ass hole! It's hard to get the sterotypes out of your brain. If a person makes a good deal on a financial transaction, he "Jewed" the guy down. Blacks are criminals. Mexicans are lazy. Irishmen are drunks. Male hairdressers are queers. Female athletes are dykes.

Another problem in our endeavor to change our thinking is that every group seems to have organizations who by their very existence promote segregation. There are groups for women, groups for every racial background, groups for every religion and for every sexual orientation. There are groups for every nationality, ie Italian Americans, Irish Americans, African Americans, etc. You name it—there's a group. These groups are accepted in our country without any reservation.

How far do you think a group would get if it was a White Male Protestant Americans organization? I have a feeling that the group would be ridiculed as being a racist organization. Yet, nothing is questioned when Congress has a "Black Caucus". Amazing isn't it?

Another problem is with Affirmative Action. Affirmative Action refers to policies that take into consideration race, color, religion, gender or national origin in order to promote a group that is underrepresented historically.

The problem is that others who may have more qualifications or experience are left behind. Affirmative Action when first used as a factor in making decisions, had a lot of merit, but some of the Civil Rights laws were enacted over 40 years ago. There comes a time, and I believe that time has passed, that one's race, color, religion, gender or national origin should not matter anymore. Qualifications and past performance should be the determining factor in the decision making process.

Will our biases and discrimination ever diminish to a point where they are no factor in our society? There is no question that people today are a lot more tolerant of individuals that don't fit the "mold". Our thinking will change over time as generations pass and our society becomes more integrated.

Gays

I didn't ask to be this way, but it just came out like that, and it's not the case—all these people say, well it's just you know, you can change from being gay to being straight. BULLSHIT! Elton John on *Biography*

In the interest of full disclosure, I have relatives who are gay. I would guess without any documentation to support my position that most people who are anti-gay don't know any outwardly gay people—or they are just ignorant bigots or more probably, both.

I believe that being gay is not a life style choice. I believe it is genetic just like a person who has a propensity to be overweight or bald, or have a bad heart or is pigeon toed. There are many studies that support that position. I once asked a gay relative if he would have chosen to be gay if he had a choice. He said, "Of course not. It would have been a lot simpler and easier to be straight".

I'm always amazed at the ignorance of some who should know better when it comes to some social issues. For example, then Senator Rick Santorum, Republican from Pennsylvania was interviewed by the Associated Press on April 7, 2003 and he indicated that homosexual acts were a threat to society and the family. No, I'm not making this up!

He further went on to say, "I have no problems with homosexuality. I have a problem with homosexual acts." Brilliant! I would imagine that he would have no problem with rape but just with the act of forced and unwanted intercourse on someone. He went on to say, "If the Supreme Court says that you have the right to consensual (gay) sex within your home, then you have the right to bigamy, you have the right to polygamy, you have the right to incest, you have the right to adultery. You have the right to anything,"

Lewis Black said it best in his Carnegie Hall concert, "Rick Santorum... eventually should be electro shocked for his own good." I know this will "shock" you. Senator Santorum lost his reelection bid in 2006 to Bob Casey, Jr 59-41%, which represented the worst defeat by a sitting Senator in over 25 years._

There are arguments against gays that are supported by religious zealots as well. They reference the Bible in support of their position that being gay is a deathly sin. They quote from Leviticus 18:22 which says, "Thou shalt not lie with mankind as with womankind; it is abomination." Later in Leviticus 20:13 it says, "If a man also lie with mankind as he lieth with a woman, both of them have committed an abomination; they shall surely be put to death; their blood shall be upon them."

Wow, pretty powerful stuff, huh? Well, the Bible says a lot of things. Here's one that I like, "Six days shall work be done, but on the seventh day there shall be to you a holy day, a sabbath of rest to the Lord; whosoever doeth work therein shall be put to death." Exodus 35:2

So, what does it all mean? Well, I have a compromise. How about this? I will agree that homosexuality is a deathly sin as soon as the religious zealots kill all the people who have ever worked on Sunday.

6. Political Parties

If you seek to be a perfect minority, you'll remain a minority Newt Gingrich, defending his endorsement of a pro-choice moderate Republican in a NY congressional race.

Political parties began as early as the birth of our country. The Federalist Party was formed by Alexander Hamilton. Hamilton was George Washington's Secretary of the Treasury. He was supported by merchants, bankers and businessmen, and he favored a fiscally sound and nationally strong government. George Washington and John Adams were Federalists.

In opposition, Patrick Henry, Sam Adams and others were deemed Anti-Federalist due to their opposition to a strong federal government and the fear that the executive would end up being a monarch. The Anti-Federalists literally died as a party as soon as the Constitution was ratified.

Subsequently, the Democratic-Republican Party came to be as the opponent of the Federalists. Led by Thomas Jefferson and James Madison, this party, mostly farmers, opposed a strong central government. Other political parties have come and gone since then, however, most were one issue parties that soon faded into history. Our form of government currently supports two major political parties. Neither party has a monopoly on good ideas although both parties would swear to differ.

The Democratic Party began in its present form with the election of President Andrew Jackson in 1828. The Republican Party was found in 1854 by the anti-slavery advocates. Its first elected President was Abraham Lincoln in 1860. The values and political positions of the parties, however, have changed over the decades since the mid 19th century.

Generally speaking, the Democratic Party is the more liberal of the two parties, but that does not mean that all Democrats are liberals. In fact, it is a center/left party. Many in the party are moderate as opposed to liberal in their views and have been dubbed as "New Democrats". They are more conservative on fiscal matters, but more progressive on social issues. Twenty-two percent of the voters describe themselves as liberals with 82% of those voting Democratic. *CNN* Exit Poll, 2008.

More than 50% of Democrats are socially progressive and favor national health care, stem cell research, and the legalization of same sex marriages. They are pro-choice on abortion, favor some gun controls and a secular government. *Pew Research Center "Beyond Red vs Blue"*, May 10, 2005. It is their belief that government can be a solution to some problems of our society.

In recent years white collar college educated professionals located in the suburbs of large cities have become more Democratic in their voting habits. In general, the Democratic Party is more inclusive of its potential members and actively seeks members of diverse cultures and opinions. The party is strongest in New England, the Mid Atlantic states, the Great Lakes States and the west coast.

The Republican Party is the more conservative of the two parties both fiscally and socially. The party is center/right. It emphasizes the free market as the driving force of our economy and abhors government interference. As President Reagan said, "Government is not a solution to our problem, government is the problem."

The party is pro-business with a large following in the financial area and that of small business owners. *"Democrats and Republicans — Rhetoric and Reality"*, Joseph Fried, New York: Algora Publishing, 2008. Church goers are more likely to vote Republican as are higher income voters. Republicans are normally very conservative on social issues of all types. Also it can be political suicide if the words "tax increase" come out of a Republican candidate's mouth.

The Republican Party at times appears to have a litmus test of its members to be accepted by the true believers. In order to be accepted by those members, the candidate must be, for example, pro-life, pro-gun and against same sex marriages.

At times, these social conservative positions tend to alienate many independents who are more moderate socially even though they are supportive in general of the Republicans on fiscal matters. As a result, a candidate has to focus the campaign so far right to get the nomination for a federal office, that he or she has problems bringing the moderates and independents into the fold for the general election. Thus the quote of Newt Gingrich, noted above.

The Republican Party is strongest in the South, Midwest and Mountain states. There are some pockets of Republican office holders in New England, however, those Republicans are considered quite moderate.

Both parties have extremists—the Democrats on the left and the Republicans on the right. While election to statewide offices or to the House or Senate can be won by extremists in certain states and districts, it is virtually impossible for anyone on the far left or right to be elected President.

For the most part, independents have final say so as to who is elected President since neither the Democrats nor the Republicans can win a majority just by relying on its own members' votes. Therefore, it is unwise for either party to nominate a member of its extreme wing to be the party's standard bearer for the presidency. In 1964, the Republicans nominated Senator Barry Goldwater for President. At the time he was considered to be too far to the right to most voters. Likewise, the Democrats did the same thing in 1972 by nominating Senator George McGovern as its candidate for President. He was perceived by the voters as being too far left. Both Goldwater and McGovern were defeated by landslide proportions in the general election.

7. Elections

We always want the best man to win an election. Unfortunately, he never runs. Will Rogers- American cowboy and social commentator.

Elections in our country are straight out of fantasy land with a twist of good versus evil. Very few issues are ever discussed, with the limited exception of presidential debates which at least focus on issues for a few minutes every four years. Even then, the issues are discussed only generally in sound bites.

All candidates for office have a platform, but it is usually hidden in the recesses of the campaign's web site. Candidates don't even go there in their speeches although they may tell you the web site address. If you travel to the web site, you most likely will fall asleep. Candidates know that if they speak in specifics about their vision of America, it will bore the hell out of any crowd. So, they ignore the issues and just speak in generalities to charm the crowd.

To win a national or even a statewide race, a candidate needs to do just a few things. First, the candidate needs to define the opponent as negatively as possible; second, the candidate needs to blame him or his political party for the problems that the country or state has; and lastly, the candidate has to scare the electorate as to what will happen if the opponent is elected. Pretty simple, and incredibly, it works a great deal of the time.

Candidates rarely focus on themselves because they might come up short in their qualifications so, they spend their money telling the voters what is wrong about their opponent. This strategy is accomplished primarily through negative advertising.

Voters have said over and over that they do not like negative campaign ads, and yet, it has been proven that they are effective and do sway enough voters to suggest negative campaigning is here to stay.

For the really big lies about a candidate, it is always good to have an independent group air the ad so that the candidate can deny any involvement in the ad. But whatever you do, don't deny the truthfulness of those ads. Let the voters decide.

As to the candidate, don't ever say exactly what you mean and for God's sake don't ever get specific on anything unless it is uncontroversial like being for Mother's Day on the second Sunday in May.

Campaign by using general terms that have positive vibes like "working class", but don't define what you mean by working class. Make the voters think you are talking to them. Use the phrase "our great country" and make sure you say at the end of every speech "… our country's best days are ahead of us…" because no one wants to think that the Chinese are kicking our ass.

Elections also involve lobbyists and special interest. There are over 17,000 lobbyists, each representing a special interest, and they have money to spend on campaigns. Lots of money. So, while the candidates are speaking to you, they are also pandering to the special interests—special interests that may represent your interest too, ie the AARP, the National Rifle Association, American Medical Association, or teacher unions. So, as a candidate, promote your special interests as good and the opponents as evil. Your lobbyists are patriots. Theirs are slime balls.

Another tactic used by candidates is very effective. Don't ever blame our country's problems on the voters, and under no circumstances do you tell the voters that they have to sacrifice. This isn't the "Greatest Generation" who sacrificed as part of the price for being Americans.

The generations alive today other than our military members, have done very little sacrificing for the good of their country and that fact doesn't look to change anytime soon.

Blame our problems on Congress or the President or the Governor, but never blame the voters who elected these guys. Newt Gingrich said it best, "People don't elect presidents who tell them to sacrifice. They elect presidents who solve problems so they don't have to sacrifice."

If candidates do what is noted above, they will be successful most of the time. Why? Because the electorate is gullible. They will believe anything if it makes them feel better.

One possible solution to clean up our election mess is to have all national and statewide elections publically funded. This would limit the influence of special interests and allow candidates to not be beholden to large contributors. Unfortunately, public funding solely in campaigns is probably unconstitutional as an interference with the right to free association.

Presidential Election of 2000

The election of 2000 was in short, a farce and a very bad representation of our society. The debacle in Florida was an embarrassment to that state. The partiality shown in the US Supreme Court decision in *Bush v Gore* was most troublesome especially coming from the highest judicial court in the land.

All we needed to do in that election was to let the Supreme Court vote for president. There were 5 Republicans and 4 Democrats on the court at the time, and surprisingly, the decision in favor of not allowing the re-count to continue in Florida, and thus certifying Republican George Bush as the winner of the election was 5-4, all votes down party lines.

Neither side's argument was consistent with past precedent, and none of the justices voted based upon their past writings. The five Republican justices voted for federal intervention in a state matter and the four Democrats did just the opposite. What a joke.

In addition, the confusion of the butterfly ballot in Florida was obvious, so much so, that even independent candidate, Patrick Buchanan admitted that the 3,000 plus votes he received in Palm Beach County, a liberal leaning county with a large Jewish population, was undoubtedly intended to be cast for Vice-President Gore.

In fairness, each vote which clearly identified the voter's intent should have been counted. Now, we will never know who was actually elected by the people. The only thing we do know is that the election of 2000 was decided by the nine justices of the Supreme Court, and the 500,000 vote majority Gore had over Bush was irrelevant.

You say what difference does it make? Well do you really think we would have made an unprovoked attack on Iraq if Al Gore was president? Do you think he would have advocated a tax cut instead of paying down the deficit? It matters…in every election.

8. Congress, The Land of Special Interest and the Home of Hypocrisy

You may fool all the people some of the time, you can even fool some of the people all of the time, but you cannot fool all of the people all the time. Abraham Lincoln

What is the number one job of a congressman or senator? To represent their district or state with the highest integrity with an eye towards doing what is best for the country? To find common ground with their colleagues to find solutions to our country's problems? No!

The number one job of a congressman or senator is to get re-elected. Job security is everything. Not yours….theirs!

So, in order to get re-elected, our Washington elected officials on Capitol Hill will do anything regardless of whether or not it is good for the country, to get re-elected. They will kiss any ass they have to and will compromise their principles to get that much needed contribution to their campaign war chests.

Here is an example. In 2009, 27 Senators co-sponsored Senate Bill 2853, The Bipartisan Task Force for Responsible Fiscal Action Act of 2009. The purpose of the bill was to form a task force to establish a long term plan for fiscal stability and economic prosperity. In essence the task force was to recommend ways to balance the budget.

Seven co-sponsors of the bill, all Republicans including John McCain, Bob Bennett, Sam Brownback, Mike Crapo, John Ensign, Kay Hutchison and James Inhofe withdrew their sponsorship in part because of pressure put on them by Grover Norquist of Americans for Tax Reform who made it clear that he would not support them in future elections if they voted for the bill. They all voted against it because of what they said was the fear the commission would support a tax hike.

Sixty votes were needed to pass the legislation. Only 54 Senators voted for it. If the seven cowards had voted for the bill, it would have passed. Norquist apparently has enough pull to scare the shit out of certain Senators and get them to change their minds in spite of their own beliefs. They caved to the pressure for their own personal survival. The country might not be fiscally responsible, but they at least saved their own hides! Nice job!

As a side note, shortly after this occurred, Evan Bayh from Indiana, another co-sponsor of the bill and a Senator who actually has a spine, decided to retire from the Senate at the end of his term in 2010. Many speculate that the failure of this bill to pass and the gutless behavior of the seven Senators was the straw that broke the camel's back leading to Senator Bayh's decision.

The Senator said in his retirement statement shortly after the vote on the bill:

> After all these years, my passion for service to my fellow citizens is undiminished, but my desire to do so by serving in Congress has waned. For some time, I have had a growing conviction that Congress is not operating as it should. There is too much partisanship and not enough progress -- too much narrow ideology and not enough practical problem-solving. Even at a time of enormous challenge, the peoples' business is not being done….

> Two weeks ago, the Senate voted down a bipartisan commission to deal with one of the greatest threats facing our nation: our exploding deficits and debt. The measure would have passed, but seven members who had endorsed the idea instead voted "no" for short-term political reasons….

> All of this and much more has led me to believe that there are better ways to serve my fellow citizens, my beloved state, and our nation than continued service in Congress.

To put it in words most people can understand: I love working for the people of Indiana, I love helping our citizens make the most of their lives, but I do not love Congress.

Every representative tells you what the problems are, and who is to blame for those problems, but very few offer solutions other than to cut waste and fraud and cut spending. Wow! What geniuses. They will never tell you what to cut or where the waste and fraud is because they have no clue where it is.

Further, telling the citizens specifics will alienate part of the electorate. Can you imagine a Republican saying , "We need to cut 15% in the Defense budget." Have you ever heard a Democrat say, "I think we could cut the deficit by eliminating some social programs."

Our representatives in Congress better not exhibit any type of independent thinking on national problems. They better not show any inclination of working towards viable solutions to our problems with a member of the opposition party. Republicans better not even suggest raising taxes and Democrats shall not suggest cutting entitlement programs.

Our elected officials in Washington have to tow the party line. If they don't, their party's leadership in the House or Senate, will threaten them with a primary challenge at the next election, and if they don't threaten them, some special interest group will. It's the them versus us philosophy. Whatever the Democrats want, the Republicans are against and vice versa. The welfare of the country and its citizens be damned! Is it any wonder that Congress' approval rating is so low.

Another reason the approval rating is so low is because of the hypocrisy of our legislators. For example in 2009, the House passed a $1.1 trillion spending bill laced with over 5000 congressional pet projects earmarked for their respective home districts. These earmarks accounted for $3.9 billion.

Here's the kicker. Some Republicans who proposed the earmarks then voted against the bill. This way they could tell their constituents they voted against the spending bill but brought home the bacon. Isn't that incredible!

You want more? The Republicans were upset because the Democrats expanded the hate crime law making it a crime to assault people because of their sexual orientation. The bill was attached to a must pass defense policy bill. Interestingly, the Republicans weren't upset when the Patriot Act was added to a must pass defense bill a few years back. Some of the Democrats were. Hypocrisy at its finest.

Republican senators, who attacked the cost of a Democratic health care bill showed far different concerns just six years previous, when they approved a major Medicare expansion that has added tens of billions of dollars to federal deficits. All GOP senators, including the 24 who voted for the 2003 Medicare expansion, oppose the health care bill that's backed by President Barack Obama and most Congressional Democrats because of its cost.

Even some conservatives can see the hypocrisy in all this. "As far as I am concerned, any Republican who voted for the Medicare drug benefit has no right to criticize anything the Democrats have done in terms of adding to the national debt," said Bruce Bartlett, an official in the administrations of Ronald Reagan and George H.W. Bush. He made his comments in a *Forbes* article titled *"Republican Deficit Hypocrisy."*

Bartlett further said the 2003 Medicare expansion was "a pure giveaway" that cost more than this year's Senate or House health bills will cost. More important, he said, "the drug benefit had no dedicated financing, no offsets and no revenue-raisers. One hundred percent of the cost simply added to the federal budget deficit. The truth comes out, but, please note, Mr Bartlett is not an officeholder so he can tell the truth.

Senate Republicans blasted a spending bill to fund the government for 2011 primarily due to earmarks added to the bill. The Republicans argued that the voters had spoken loudly in the 2010 election against funding these earmarks. In fact, Republican House and Senate members had vowed to ban these earmarks when Congress returned in 2011. Senate Minority Leader, Mitch McConnell of Kentucky, said, "This is exactly what the American people said…they did not want us to do." He said he would fight the measure in the year end session of Congress, and further indicated, "I am actively working to defeat it."

Now, here's the kicker. Included in the proposed earmarks was a $1.5 million wastewater project as well as others proposed by, you guessed it, Senator Mitch McConnell! When asked about his own projects, Senator McConnell said his projects were requested before the Republicans voted to ban them. Are you kidding me?

But that doesn't top Senator John Thune of South Dakota. He decided that he would not vote for the tax compromise at the end of 2010 because of earmarks in the bill. Earmarks that he put in the bill? Only $65 million worth.

Lastly, let's give it up for the Tea Party Caucus. This Congressional caucus states that it is in favor of cutting government spending. Yet, of its 52 members, 36 requested hundreds of earmarks in fiscal 2010 totaling over a billion dollars. This includes Congressman Denny Rehberg of Montana, who is the leader of the pack. He requested along with some other co-sponsors, 88 earmark projects totaling over $100 million in fiscal 2010. With respect to spending, he said this in an e-mail from his office, "It's easy to be a member of the TEA Party Caucus because, like them, I agree that we're Taxed Enough Already and we've got to balance the budget by cutting spending instead of raising taxes. Deficit spending is not new, but the unprecedented rate of spending in Congress is. Montanans have tightened their belts, and it's way past time for Congress to follow their lead. The TEA Party Caucus is about listening to concerned Americans who want to fundamentally change how Congress spends their tax dollars. On that, we're in total agreement." Glad to hear that, Congressman.

Back in the 1950's, then Senator John F Kennedy wrote a book entitled *Profiles in Courage*. The book was about eight US Senators who took unpopular but correct stands on certain issues of their times. The premise of the book was to show the courage taken by the Senators at the time. The current crop of Congressmen and Senators for the most part do a great deal of profiling themselves but show very little courage in taking stands for the good of the country.

Maybe we need important decisions made by a binding committee appointed by Congress since no one in Congress has the courage to make a decision that may have a negative effect on their ability to get re-elected.

Maybe then we could actually have a serious body making important and proper decisions about our future survival.

It is interesting to note that in spite of Congress' low approval rating as a body, there is a relatively small turnover rate, especially in the House. It appears that generally voters blame Congress for our problems but don't blame their own Congressman.

There simply is too much grandstanding among Congress members with very little actually getting done for the people. Whoever is in power can't govern because the minority's main job appears to be to obstruct anything the majority is for rather than attempting compromise for the good of the country.

It is possible that responsible governing can actually occur when the executive and congress are run by different parties. For example when Ronald Reagan was President, his negatives were higher than Obama's after his first year in office, but when he and Democratic Speaker of the House Tip O'Neill sat down and used a pragmatic approach to governing, the country did much better, and Reagan was re-elected. Same can be said about President Clinton and Speaker Gingrich.

Here's the problem. Congress is too polarizing, especially in the House. We have elected too many left and right wing nuts. They are in the minority when considering the entire electorate, but in the halls of Congress, they can easily have their voices heard and they make every effort to control their party's agenda. There are so few moderate Republicans or conservative Democrats as there were in years past.

Our country's Presidents are elected by the independents, the center, if you will. Yet because of the "wing nuts", the country is having a hard time governing in the center. The left wing brands Bush as a right wing tax cutter who only cares about the rich. The right wing counters by calling Obama a socialist. Both extremists are wrong. Our Congress needs to get back to the center where decisions get made and rhetoric is subdued. Otherwise Congress may become irrelevant if it isn't already.

9. Why We Went to War with Iraq

My answer is bring 'em on. —President George W. Bush, challenging militants attacking U.S. forces in Iraq, July 2, 2003

Saddam Hussein was a bad man who tortured his citizens and murdered his political enemies. He was, however, no worse than a handful of other madmen running countries in the world who are no threat to the United States.

So why did we go to war? On March 21, 2006, President Bush was asked by White House Correspondent Helen Thomas why.

HELEN THOMAS: I'd like to ask you, Mr. President, your decision to invade Iraq has caused the deaths of thousands of Americans and Iraqis, wounds of Americans and Iraqis for a lifetime. Every reason given, publicly at least, has turned out not to be true. My question is, why did you really want to go to war? From the moment you stepped into the White House, from your Cabinet -- your Cabinet officers, intelligence people, and so forth -- what was your real reason? You have said it wasn't oil -- quest for oil, it hasn't been Israel, or anything else. What was it?

PRESIDENT GEORGE W. BUSH: I think your premise, in all due respect to your question and to you as a lifelong journalist, is that, you know, I didn't want war. To assume I wanted war is just flat wrong, Helen, in all due respect --

HELEN THOMAS: Everything --

PRESIDENT GEORGE W. BUSH: Hold on for a second, please.

HELEN THOMAS: -- everything I've heard --

PRESIDENT GEORGE W. BUSH: Excuse me, excuse me. No president wants war. Everything you may have heard is that, but it's just simply not true. My attitude about the defense of this country changed on September the 11th. We -- when we got attacked, I vowed then and there to use every asset at my disposal to protect the American people. Our foreign policy changed on that day, Helen. You know, we used to think we were secure because of oceans and previous diplomacy, but we realized on September the 11th, 2001, that killers could destroy innocent life. And I'm never going to forget it. And I'm never going to forget the vow I made to the American people that we will do everything in our power to protect our people.

Part of that meant to make sure that we didn't allow people to provide safe haven to an enemy. And that's why I went into Iraq -- hold on for a second --

HELEN THOMAS: They didn't do anything to you or to our country.

PRESIDENT GEORGE W. BUSH: Look -- excuse me for a second, please. Excuse me for a second. They did. The Taliban provided safe haven for al-Qaeda. That's where al-Qaeda trained --

HELEN THOMAS: I'm talking about Iraq --

PRESIDENT GEORGE W. BUSH: Helen, excuse me. That's where -- Afghanistan provided safe haven for al-Qaeda. That's where they trained. That's where they plotted. That's where they planned the attacks that killed thousands of innocent Americans.
I also saw a threat in Iraq. I was hoping to solve this problem diplomatically. That's why I went to the Security Council; that's why it was important to pass 1441, which was unanimously

passed. And the world said, 'Disarm, disclose, or face serious consequences' –

HELEN THOMAS: -- go to war --

PRESIDENT GEORGE W. BUSH: -- and therefore, we worked with the world, we worked to make sure that Saddam Hussein heard the message of the world. And when he chose to deny inspectors, when he chose not to disclose, then I had the difficult decision to make to remove him. And we did, and the world is safer for it.

So, do you know now why we went to war? Neither do I.

On February 20, 2011, former Defense Secretary, Donald Rumsfeld indicated in an interview with Candy Crowley of *CNN's "State of the Union"* that there were many reasons for invading Iraq but the big reason for going to war with Iraq was because of intelligence reports indicating that Iraq possessed weapons of mass destruction. Asked if the United States would not have invaded if our leaders had known that there were no WMD, Rumsfeld stated, "I think that's probably right."

Right up to the beginning of the war in March, 2003 United Nation inspectors could find no evidence of the weapons. The United States went to the UN Security Council seeking a resolution to allow the use of force in Iraq but the resolution was defeated due to lack of evidence of the weapons existing in Iraq and the questionable intelligence leading the United States position.

The "questionable intelligence" was in part based upon a CIA operative in Iraq later identified as Rafid Ahmed Alwan al-Janabi. He falsely represented that in 1999 he worked in a plant that manufactured biological weapons as part of Iraq's weapons of mass destruction program.

Bush using this information in his State of the Union address in 2003, stated, "we know that Iraq, in the late 1990s, had several mobile biological weapons labs." In spite of the defeated resolution and questionable intelligence gathering, the United States invaded Iraq. In 2008, the US Senate's Intelligence Committee found that the Bush Administration had "misrepresented the intelligence and the threat from Iraq."

In an interview with the *Guardian* in February, 2011, al-Janabi, "admitted for the first time that he lied about his story, then watched in shock as it was used to justify the war." Bush and Vice-President Dick Cheney both admitted later that there were no weapons of mass destruction in Iraq. Bush later stated that the intelligence failure in Iraq was his biggest regret of his Presidency. *Iraq and weapons of mass destruction-Wikipedia Encyclopedia* footnoted.

As of May, 2010 there were over 4400 of our soldiers killed in action with an additional 32,000 injured due to this faulty intelligence. *Casualties of the War-Wikipedia Encyclopedia* footnoted.

10. Our Uninformed Citizenry

The key to life is to be smart enough to know what you don't know.
This Author paraphrasing parts of the quote which have appeared
in various forms in the past.

Boy, are people ever dumb. Well maybe not dumb, but certainly ignorant
about current events and affairs of state. They don't think they are, but
they are. Carpenters are expert in their trade. Dentists are experts in their
profession. Engineers are experts in their chosen fields. No one would
think for a minute to question any of these people about their work unless
that person was also of the same field. So, why do so many people feel they
are experts in how to run this country or what is the best way to handle
foreign affairs? It's mind boggling.

On the whole, people don't have a clue about what they are talking about when
it comes to affairs of state. They run their mouth off about things that they
haven't even researched. They repeat things that their friends told them.

Some of their opinions are based upon biased reporting of radio or television
political shows hosted by men and women who have their own separate
agenda (usually to keep their ratings up and/or to sell books). The truth
is of no concern to these pundits. They twist innuendo and half truths to
make their points. They prey upon people's fears and prejudices and have
no problem stereotyping groups.

And some of the public buys it, hook, line and sinker. As such, those who
are informed only by those who spout this crap serve no purpose at all other
than to expand more misinformation by way of mouth, internet or e-mail.

Always consider the source of the opinion. Who is more credible? Who has an agenda? Who has bias or prejudice?

People hear something and believe it without ever considering the situations that may have arisen leading to the reported incident. People are basically gullible and are too lazy to do their own research but instead believe the most idiotic things.

A recent poll indicated that nearly 47% of the people believe President Obama signed the T.A.R.P. (Troubled Asset Relief Program) legislation, and therefore blame him for bailing out the banks The Act was signed by President Bush on October 3, 2008, one month before the election of Obama and three and a half months before he became President. Only 34% correctly indicated that the act was signed by President Bush. *Pew Research Center* Poll, reported by David Weigel, *www.slate.com* August 11, 2010.

According to *Public Policy Polling*, 33% of New Jersey Republicans think that Obama was not born in the US. Incredibly, 18% of conservatives think Obama is the Anti-Christ. On the Democratic side of idiocy, 32% believe President Bush had advanced warning of 9/11. *Newsweek*, Jonathan Alter, September 28, 2009.

According to a *Pew Research Center* poll as reported in the *Fort Wayne Journal-Gazette* on August 20, 2010, 18% of the public still believe Obama is a Muslim.

Anna Quindlen of Newsweek in her February 8, 2009, column noted:

> One poll of former Obama supporters who abandoned the Democrats in Massachusetts showed that 41 percent of those who opposed the health-care plan weren't sure exactly why. If elected officials are supposed to act based on the wisdom of ordinary people, they're going to need ordinary people to be wiser than that.

A recent *Kaiser Health Tracking* poll as reported in September, 2010, found that 30% of all seniors over 65 still believe that government panels, ie death squads, can make end of life decisions with respect to those who are covered by Medicare.

My educated guess is that a fair amount of our uninformed citizenry still believes that Iraq had weapons of mass destruction and was somehow involved in the attacks of September 11, 2001. This in spite of the fact that both President Bush and Vice-President Cheney have admitted that there was no evidence of these weapons being present in Iraq. They, of course, blamed everything on faulty intelligence in spite of UN intelligence to the contrary.

Americans want less taxes and less government but at the same time they want things done. They vote for candidates who espouse change and then turn against their candidate when he or she tries to implement change.

Our citizens have an unreasonable expectation of what government can or cannot do. Here is what Americans desire. They want problems solved but they don't want to sacrifice to have those problems solved. They want cuts in spending as long as it doesn't affect them. They vote against millages for schools and then wonder why programs get cancelled in the schools. In essence, people want services but they don't want to pay for them.

In a recent poll, adults were asked, "Would you be willing to pay higher taxes to help reduce the federal budget deficit?" Not surprisingly 71% said no and only 20% said yes. *Rasmussen Reports*, March13-14, 2011 Survey of 1000 adults.

Citizens think that the government can just make unemployment go away and solve our immigration problem by building a fence. Guess what? It cost money to do this. The ignorance of our citizens doesn't end there.

When it comes to serious questions of governing and making tough choices, they rarely have a clue. A 2010 *World Public Opinion* poll found that citizens believe that a good way of lowering our budget deficit is to cut foreign aid from what they believe is its current level of 27%, to a more reasonable 13%. The actual current budget spends less than 1% on foreign affairs! *Newsweek, How Dumb Are We?* March 28, 2011.

You read the results of these polls and you wonder what the hell is going on with the citizens of this country. Can they be that ignorant? Apparently, yes! Our citizens praise or criticize bills or passed legislation without ever reading or researching what the legislation says. It's like a carpenter who would build a house without any architectural drawings. It's insane! So who are we dealing with? Here's my take on it.

Basically there are five types of people when it comes to current events and problems of society. First are the people who simply do not care about current events. These are the people who don't vote, don't read the newspaper, don't watch news on TV and simply have no idea what is going on. They also have no opinions about the issues of the day. They are the type of people that will hear someone spout off about some issue, and just agree with the person rather than take a stand or confront the person. These people are ignorant but harmless in that they have no influence on the way the country runs or the direction in which it is going. They don't vote—ever.

Second are people who have many opinions based solely upon what they have heard other people say. They have never thought out any issue on their own or even researched any issue. They hardly ever vote and probably aren't even registered, but they like to talk a good game. For the most part, these people are followers who are easily lead.

Third are people who have very strong opinions based upon their own biases, prejudices or religious beliefs. They tend to get most of their information from e-mails authored by people with no interest in the truth or from right/left wing radio or television programs. Rather than thinking the issue through or researching it, they just believe whatever they hear that is consistent with their biases, prejudices or religious beliefs and disregard anything to the contrary. These people vote sometimes, and when they do vote, it is as much against a candidate as for his or her opponent. They might be able to tell you why they don't like a candidate but they probably cannot tell you why they do like the candidate that they vote for.

Fourth are those who are one issue people. They really don't care what a candidate stands for as long as he or she is pro-choice, pro-life, pro-guns, pro-gun control, for or against social issues, etc. These people always vote and are passionate about their one issue.

Fifth are those who do keep up with society issues by reading and watching news programs. They are smart enough to know that very few issues are cut and dried but in fact have strong arguments on both sides of the issues. They can see the issues and can separate the facts from the fiction. They do not let fear mongering or biases and prejudices enter into their thinking. They do have strong opinions but they are based upon sound reasoning. These are the people who should run the country and choose its leaders. The others should stick to what they know, and stay away from political issues.

11. E-Mail Misinformation

He who knows nothing is closer to the truth than he whose mind is filled with falsehoods and errors. Thomas Jefferson

I know people who do not hesitate forwarding asinine e-mails over the internet without checking or researching the information to see if it is even remotely true. Some of these e-mails are vicious, libelous and baseless. They are easily determined to be false by doing a cursory word search. These word searches may take up to two or three minutes to do which in some cases is quicker than actually reading the e-mail.

The internet is a vast sea of information which can be accessed by our fingertips. We can almost without exception verify or discard rumors or information in a matter of minutes. So why don't the senders do so before they hit the forward and send buttons? I suppose one of the reasons is they want to believe the misinformation is actually true because of their hostile feelings about the person or subject matter of the e-mail.

Here are some examples of the lies I have received.

- During the 2008 campaign, Obama wanted to raise taxes for capital gains and profit on all home sales.

- Democrat Presidents being responsible for starting World War II, the Korean War and the Vietnam War.

- According to the Book of Revelations, the Anti-Christ will be a male Muslim in his 40's, ie. Obama.

- The late actor, Lee Marvin was a marine on Iwo Jima and was awarded the Navy Cross for heroism, and right beside him on Mt Suribachi was none other than Capt Kangaroo, Bob Keeshan.

- Mr Rogers of Mr Rogers Neighborhood fame was a Navy SEAL in Vietnam and had 25 kills in combat.

- Sarah Palin's baby with Down's Syndrome is really Bristol's child.

- In 20 years there will be enough Muslims in the United States to elect a Muslim President.

- Then Senator Obama saying on the television news program *Meet the Press*, on September 7, 2008, in response to a question asked of him by General Bill Ginn that his wife disrespects the flag and they have attended many flag burning ceremonies. This was reported by *Washington Post* columnist Dale Lindsborg.

- The Democratic Congress bailed out AIG because AIG insures the trust fund for congressional pensions

- Obama wanted our servicemen and women to pay for their own health insurance to cover them for war wounds.

- Charlie Reese, a reporter for the *Orlando Sentinel,* wrote an article going after Congress, the President and the Supreme Court for their incompetence in governing. The article also goes after the Speaker of the House, Nancy Pelosi, for having the gall for attacking the President on the deficit which in fact was created by the House. He indicates that if we are in Iraq, it's because those currently governing want us in Iraq.

Now, the truth:

- Obama wanted to raise the capital gains tax to levels which would still be lower than they were when Reagan was President for those whose income is over $250,000 only.

- The Japanese started World War II against the United States by attacking us at Pearl Harbor. Germany declared war against us within a few days thereafter. The Korean War was started by North Korea. Our involvement in the Vietnam War started when Eisenhower, a Republican, was President.

- Revelations doesn't even mention the "Anti-Christ", and the Muslim religion did not even begin until 400 years after Revelations was written. Mayor Danny Funderburk of Fort Mill, South Carolina received a great deal of negative publicity for circulating this e-mail. He said he did it because he was curious if there was any scriptural support for the accusations. Seriously, that's what he said!

- Lee Marvin was not on Iwo Jima and never was awarded the Navy Cross. Capt Kangaroo, while in the service, never saw action in World War II.

- Mr Rogers was never in the service.

- I trust someone reputable would come out with proof of the Palin baby not being Sarah's if it were so.

- The math on this isn't even close. In order to do this the Muslim population would have to double every 3 ½ years, every Muslim would have to vote for the Muslim candidate and there could not be any non-Muslim births in this country for the entire 20 years. Wow!

- Obama and the General were not even on Meet the Press that day, Thomas Friedman and Joe Biden were, and there has never been a reporter for the *Washington Post* or any other newspaper named Dale Lindsborg.

- The Federal Reserve and Treasury Department lead by Republican Secretary Henry Paulsen bailed out AIG, not the Congress. Also, the Trust Fund is not insured by any company.

- Who in their right mind would ever believe this? Not even Fox News has reported this nonsense.

- The article was written in the 1980's when Ronald Reagan was President. The Senate was controlled by the Republicans and, Nancy Pelosi was not even a member of the House of Representatives at the time. Obviously, we were not in Iraq either. Reese retired in 2001 so, it appears that his piece has been creatively changed since that time by someone else.

How about innuendo and half truths? I got those too. I have received the following e-mails:

- Trying to show how Hitler and Obama had similar upbringing

- Norman Thomas, a socialist, stated in 1944, that he did not need to run for President on the Socialist ticket since the Democrats had already adopted his platform.

- A response to an Editorial written by Cindy Williams in the *Washington Times* wherein she objected to military pay raises of 13% as being more than the military deserved. Williams was an Assistant Director for National Security in the Congressional Budget Office under the Obama administration. It is suggested by a young Air Force member that she should join a group deploying to Afghanistan and see the families that they leave behind to see if she might change her mind. It is noted that although he disagrees with her opinion, he will fight to the death in Kabul to write it.

- A request to sign, no matter what you think of Obama, a petition against illegal immigrants receiving Social Security benefits. The petition says that the Senate has already passed the measure and that we should encourage President Obama to veto it if the bill passes the House of Representatives. Benefits should only go to our citizens. The petition is followed by a form letter to President Obama and over 900 hundred names listed in support.

And the truth is:

- One murdered six million Jews, started a world war which lead to thousands of deaths, and placed 10 to 12 year old boys on the front lines when the war was hopelessly lost. I pointed out to the person who sent me this that if she would have printed this in Nazi Germany, she probably would have been executed. Her response to me was comical. She said that she agreed with me and said that it just goes to show you what some people will do to get things started. So why did she contribute to what she was against? She probably did not see the irony of her own comments.

- Thomas actually said that both the Democrats and the Republicans have adopted a socialistic agenda.

- The editorial was written by Cindy Williams in the *Washington Post*, not *Times*, but it was written in January, 2000, long before we were in any war. She, therefore never worked for President Obama . She was, in fact, a senior research fellow at MIT. Also, she was objecting to a 25% increase coming just after the military had received another 5% raise. So why did the Airman mention Afghanistan? Because someone decided that the e-mail would be much better if they made some changes to his letter to make it look like it was current and thus, make the Obama administration look bad.

- The petition was sent in 2006, and was originally sent to President Bush. So, again, someone thought it would be fun to change the President from Bush to Obama. Oh, and by the way, the Senate never voted for such a change to the Social Security Act...ever!

The e-mail network also has some very idiotic comments about what should be done in this country to make it better. In short, it is suggested that we should just tell the rest of the world to go to hell. We should isolate ourselves, perhaps like North Korea. Of course, none of the ideas are well thought out or proposed by anyone with any experience or significant intelligence from which to advocate these positions.

What's really scary is the authors of these e-mails and those who keep circulating them are allowed to vote. Most of them probably don't, but if one does, it's one too many. They probably shouldn't operate farm machinery either.

12. Women in Power

We still think of a powerful man as a born leader and a powerful woman as an anomaly. Margaret Atwood-Poet

Throughout American history men have dominated the leadership and power positions in society. Women for the most part have been relegated to second class status with very little hope of achieving success outside the family unit. They couldn't even vote until 1920.

This all changed in the latter part of the twentieth century. Women began attending college in mass majoring in areas considered to be "male only". Business, law, math and science became more common choices for women than ever before. Girls were raised to prepare for careers outside the home. Being a spouse and mother was put on hold.

This societal change could be seen everywhere from private industry to governmental service. Women were not only joining the ranks of the professional workforce, but also having positions of authority in which they were making decisions--big decisions that affected our lives every day.

Most families welcomed the change in society, and encouraged their daughters to pursue their goals and dreams by attending college and grad schools. The transition in private industry and boardrooms seems to be positive for the most part...at least the conflicts if any, have not been as publically broadcasted as they were at the beginning of the transition of women from the home to the professional workforce.

This much needed change has not been as swift in the political arena. The public independently and through the media, have scorched women that have political power. This heat comes mostly from the far right and far left pundits on the radio and television and by morons who send defamatory emails to everyone in their address book. Can you think of one female national political figure that is viewed more favorably than unfavorably? Neither can I.

Let's name them. You can count them on one hand...Hillary Clinton, Nancy Pelosi and Sarah Palin!

Some issues are fair game--their qualifications, their positions on issues to name a few, but the extent of the hatred that some have for these three women is unbelievable. They attack them for the most insignificant reasons that have absolutely no relevancy to their ability to govern or to their beliefs.

These vicious attacks do not necessarily take place against Congresswomen or female Senators, unless they are in leadership roles, such as Nancy Pelosi. The vitriol also seems to subside once a person is removed from the daily national spotlight. For example, Hillary Clinton's positives in polls have increased since becoming Secretary of State. Why? I submit it's because of the fact that she's not on the news every night. Sarah Palin's negatives continue to rise or hold steady as she attempts to stay in the national spotlight.

These three women are tough as nails, and some people, both male and female, do not like aggressive women.

Men who are tough are considered leaders. Women who are tough are sometimes branded as bitches. The number of women climbing the corporate ladder and knocking down doors in Washington and in state houses is only going to increase. It is time for those still living in the Stone Age to wake up or get out of the way of this progress.

13. Balancing the Budget

Anybody in elected office would love nothing more than to give everybody tax cuts, not cut services, make sure I'm providing help to student loans, make sure that we're keeping our roads safe and our bridges safe, and make sure that we're paying for veterans who are coming back from Iraq and Afghanistan. At some point, the numbers just don't work. President Obama at the town hall meeting on *CNBC*, September 20, 2010.

We need to get spending under control and cut the "waste, fraud and abuse" in the budget. Stop it. I can't take it. Every time I hear a politician say that I want to pull out my hair.

I do not claim to be an expert in this area, but I do have some common sense comments to make. If you spend more than you take in, that's bad! How about that? I'm a genius.

There are only three ways to balance the budget- raise taxes, cut spending or do both. You do not balance the budget by cutting taxes and increasing spending. Since this is obvious, why does Congress do both? Stop me if you've heard this before---they do it to get re-elected. No one wants to hear that their taxes are going up, nor do they want to hear that due to cuts in the budget, they won't get those jobs which would be created by the funding because Congress cut the spending bill that was going to fund the project. Isn't it much easier for Congress to say funding has been approved for your project and your taxes won't have to be raised to fund it?

President GW Bush and Congress actually did that. In fact, when Bush was President, government spending rose more rapidly than at any time since Lyndon Johnson's Great Society. So, what did he do about it? He cut taxes!! *The Battle for America, 2008, pp.232-233.*

Before President Bush signed the 2003 tax cuts, the nonpartisan *Economic Policy Institute (EPI)* released a statement signed by ten Nobel prize laureates entitled *"Economists' Statement Opposing the Bush Tax Cuts"*, which stated:

> Passing these tax cuts will worsen the long-term budget outlook, adding to the nation's projected chronic deficits. This fiscal deterioration will reduce the capacity of the government to finance Social Security and Medicare benefits as well as investments in schools, health, infrastructure, and basic research. Moreover, the proposed tax cuts will generate further inequalities in after-tax income.

The *Huffington Post noted* on August 3, 2010, that the Bush era tax cut was the largest contributor to the deficit and would continue to be for many years in the future.

When President Obama took office, the federal deficit was $1.3 trillion. How do we know this? Because Vice-President Biden has said it every chance he had. The tax cuts were to expire on December 31, 2010. So what happened when the tax cuts expired? The crazies in Congress extended the tax cuts for two more years.

The Republicans wanted the tax cuts for those making more than $250,000 per year to be extended and the Democrats wanted those making less than that amount to continue receiving the tax cut. So, what the hell…let's give it to everyone. Obama signed the bill.

Congress approving the tax cut extension and Obama signing same will add $858 billion to the deficit in the next two years per Alan Simpson, co-leader of the Deficit Commission appointed by President Obama.

Congress saying it wants to balance the budget is a joke! The members simply do not have the willpower or courage to do so. Too many people will be upset by the tax increases or the spending cuts. Those people might vote for someone else in the next election. Losing their job is the biggest fear of anyone in Congress.

On March 8, 2010, Fareed Zakaria wrote an interesting column in *Newsweek*. In it he indicated that that the big fix needed to get our country back on the road to fiscal responsibility was to attack the debt. He gave three proposals to "defuse the debt bomb."

First, the country should adopt a value-added tax, ie a national sales tax at 18%. According to Leonard Burman in the *University of Virginia Tax Review*, if the sales tax rate was 25%, revenues would be large enough to balance the budget, pay for health care expansion and eliminate income taxes for all those earning less than $100,000. This would cover 90% of the households. Top tax rates for those earning more than $100,000 would be 25%, which is less than the current rate. This tax would also restrain our citizens from over consuming and reward them for saving.

Second, according to Zakaria, the country needs to eliminate subsidies for home ownership, health care and agriculture, which costs the government about $250 billion per year, by eliminating the interest deduction on mortgages, tax exemptions for employer based health plans and farm subsidies to the huge agribusinesses.

Third, adjustments need to be made to entitlements by tying benefits to rises in income, not wages. We need to raise the retirement age and link it to life expectancy.

Now, having reviewed the above, what chance do you think any of the three proposals have of passing Congress? None. Zilch. Nada. Why? Because it would be painful to all citizens, lobbyists would stop giving money to candidates, and no one in Washington would promote anything that could interfere with their chances of re-election.

Wasteful Government Spending

This is another phrase that members of Congress like to use. Here's the problem. Let's say a Congressman in California wants to earmark $100 million to his or her state or district for repairing a number of bridges. This earmark will put to work 300 people from numerous contractors and subcontractors. Obviously, these 300 will enjoy the benefit of being paid for their work and will spend their earnings on goods and services provided by their area businesses. Sounds worthwhile doesn't it? Is that earmark wasteful spending to California? No. Is it to North Dakota citizens who will not receive any benefit from the repaired bridges? Yes.

How about cutting the defense budget? Okay, let's cut $100 million. Let's say that $100 million would have been used to keep a military base open in Texas, to buy tanks and to repave an airplane runway on the base. So by cutting the defense budget by the amount noted, the Defense Department has put employees of the tank factory and paving company out of their jobs. Likewise some of the small businesses around the closed base whose principal means of income was purchases of their goods and services by the servicemen and women of the base will lose their jobs and businesses. Is that wasteful government spending? Not to the good people of the Texas area where the base was. Is it wasteful government spending to the people of New Hampshire? Probably.

As you can see, one man's wasteful government spending is another man's job!

Our citizens are all over the place when they speak their collective minds about spending. A January, 2011, *CNN* poll found that while 71% of voters wanted smaller government, the vast majority did not want cuts to Medicare, Social Security or Medicaid. What did they want to cut? Are you ready for this? WASTE!!!

According to a 2009 *Gallup Poll*, our citizens believe that waste constitutes about 50% of our government spending. *Newsweek, How Dumb Are We?* March 28, 2011. Can you say "Fantasy World"? Sure you can.

Some wish for the good old days when Ronald Reagan was President. Ronald Reagan lowered income tax rates in 1981 and 1986. Being pragmatic, however, he also raised taxes, albeit not income taxes, in 1982 and 1984. These tax increases constituted the biggest tax increase ever enacted during peacetime. Reagan reduced tax loopholes and reduced various federal tax breaks which affected mostly the higher earning citizens and businesses who had supported him. He also signed off on Social Security reform which accelerated an increase in the payroll tax rate in 1983. Government spending increased 69% during his Presidency.

With the current state of the Republican party being so conservative, it is unlikely that Reagan could get his party's nomination if he were alive today.

By the way, of the recent past two term presidents, other than Reagan's 69% increase, GW Bush increased spending by 68% and Clinton by 32%. *Bradenton Herald,* Steve Thomma, March 8, 2009.

The Tea Party

The recent political Tea Party movement has become popular to many Americans within the last few years. In 2010, they supported many candidates who adhere to the Tea Party philosophy of lower government spending.

The movement has now moved some in the House of Representatives to form a Tea Party caucus in Congress to show support for the movement.

Here's the funny part. There are 52 House members, all Republican, who are also Tea Party caucus members. In fiscal year 2010, 36 of them requested 764 earmarks in legislation totaling over $1 billion. *Citizens Against Government Waste's Pig Book,* by Reid Wilson, the *National Journal,* December 2, 2010.

Have I mentioned "Hypocrisy" before? I thought so.

14. Health Care

To our seniors, I have a message for you: you're going to die sooner.
–Sen. Tom Coburn (R- Okla.), on what will happen if health care
reform passes, Dec. 1, 2009

Political polls are all over the place when it comes to the new Health
Care law signed by President Obama. I think that is extremely interesting
because my bet is that at least 98% of those polled have never read the law
and probably more than half have never even read a summary of the law.
Yet they have an opinion. Makes you wonder what the opinion is based
upon, doesn't it?

Here's what I do know about health care in America. According to *Harper's*
Magazine as reported in the *Fort Wayne Journal-Gazette* on September 12,
2009, since 2002 the average premium for health insurance has gone up
87%. The top ten insurance company profits for that same time period
have risen 428%.

Being an investor, I certainly have no problem with companies making a
profit, but you have to pause and ponder those statistics. So what do we
get for our premiums? Certainly the United States does provide excellent
care for those who have health insurance coverage available to them. We
have approximately 267 doctors for every 100,000 people in our country,
far more than most countries. However, this is not the highest ratio in
the world. Cuba, of all places, has approximately 591 doctors per 100,000
people. The United States is not even in the top 30 in that regard. *www.
infoplease.com.*

It is very difficult to assess each country's health care for its citizens, but
according to a World Health Report published in 2000 by the *World*

Health Organization, the United States ranks 37th in the world as to its health care system. The report did note that the United States did come in First in one category—the portion of its gross domestic product going towards health care, ie we have the most expensive health care system in the world. *Fort Wayne Journal-Gazette* editorial *"The Debunker: Best health care"* September 4, 2009

With respect to the new law signed by President Obama, I don't pretend to know every detail and I certainly am not qualified to state whether it is a good law or a bad one. (Unlike those who gave opinions to pollsters) I have read many summaries of the law and I do find some aspects of the law to be an improvement.

Health plans now must cover pre-existing conditions for children and beginning in 2014, pre-existing conditions for adults. Preventative benefits must be covered at 100%. Lifetime maximums have been eliminated. I really don't see how anyone could be against those changes.

What we don't know is the ultimate cost of health care. Will it be worse or better than costs today? Let's face it. Costs are out of control. As noted above, our premiums keep going up and our deductibles keep increasing.

In addition, we pay for the uninsured. Emergency rooms are required under the law to treat all people who come to them regardless of their ability to pay. Federal and state governments help pay for those services as do insurance companies who are then charged more for the services of their insureds. *How Do Taxpayers Pay for the Uninsured, www.ehow.com* Jamie Wilson, April 3, 2010.

So, we are paying for the uninsured anyway either through our taxes or our premiums.

Something must be done. Maybe the new law will help. Those who say that it will pay for itself may be right.

Those that condemn the law, may be right as well. It is simply too early to tell.

15. Education

The foundation of every state is the education of its youth. Diogenes
Laertius--Biographer of Greek Philosophers

Our education system is in shambles. We spend too much time worrying
about whether we are going to hurt Johnny's feelings by holding him
back when we should be spending more time and effort rewarding those
who achieve by challenging them. Let's get the kids geared to what their
aptitude tells us is in their best interest and try not to just pass them
through the system.

The curriculum needs to be revamped. Do we really need Latin, German
and French taught in our secondary schools? Shouldn't we be teaching
Japanese, Chinese or Farsi? Shouldn't we start advanced math and science
classes earlier in the grades? Reading should be a top priority in the first
few years of school. Shouldn't our school year be lengthened and our school
days extended like other countries that are beating us in reading, math
and science?

How about No Child Left Behind (Bush) and Race to the Top (Obama)?
Are these programs helping? Both programs apparently place test scores as
the measure of a successful educational environment. Teachers and their
futures are on the line based upon these test scores. School officials in
many districts and states now plan to use test scores in their evaluations
of teachers.

What about the parents' responsibility? Apparently it's irrelevant. Should
a student be homeless, ill, hungry, or chronically absent from school, that
also is not factored in to the measure of success equation. *Obama's War on
Schools*, Diane Ravitch, *Newsweek*, March 28, 2011.

So, there you have it. It's all about the test scores. Some districts have even been forced to reduce classroom time for art, music, history, literature, foreign language, geography and physical education to devote more time to preparation for the state tests. Something's wrong. I wish I had the answers.

Sex education is another issue. In recent polls nearly 90% of all people polled felt the need for sex education in school. The issue is whether the emphasis should be on contraception or abstinence. Congress has poured $1.5 Billion into programs which teach abstinence. The problem is it doesn't work. A study done by the Dept of Health & Human Services during the Bush administration showed that teenagers who took abstinence-only classes were just as likely to have sex as those who didn't.

In fact, abstinence only programs may be counterproductive. Studies have shown that adolescents in abstinence only programs were less likely to use contraceptives.

Texas leads the nation in spending for abstinence only programs and it also has one of the highest teen birth rates in the country. Anna Quindlen, *Newsweek*, March 16, 2009. A growing number of states are actually turning down money from the government for abstinence only education.

Funding of education is also an issue. It seems like state budget cuts start with education. This is due primarily because students and their families have very little political power. The power is with older people who contribute to politician fund raisers and the AARP with the power it has as a lobbying organization. The funding of education is not a major concern to the elderly, and therefore, state funding goes to other programs or in tax cuts.

Cuts also affect teacher salaries. If we were to raise teacher salaries to the levels of other high paying professionals, those increases might attract more top students to the teaching profession. A few generations ago, women, due in part to gender discrimination, chose the teaching and nursing professions almost exclusively. Now, many of the top female students avoid the profession because of the low pay and seek other higher paying professions in business, medicine, law or engineering.

This position was confirmed in a recent newspaper column. In 1970, in New York City, a new teacher's starting salary in the public schools was only about $2,000 less than the salary of a starting lawyer in a law firm. Today the spread is $115,000. *McKinsey & Company, "Closing the Talent Gap"*. The study also found that currently 47% of teachers in K-12th grades scored in the bottom third on their SAT scores.

The same study found that some other countries who continue to outperform the United States in educational performance treat their teachers differently both in pay and respect. In Singapore and South Korea, teachers are placed in the profession only if they place in the top third of their peers. They are highly respected and are paid on average more than lawyers and engineers. *"Pay Teachers More"*, Nicholas Kristof, *New York Times*, March 15, 2011.

Higher funding of education, however, does not necessarily correlate with student achievement in our country. In 2009, the states that had the highest SAT scores of college bound seniors were Iowa, Illinois, Minnesota, Missouri and South Dakota. Per pupil spending in those states was not ranked high at all. Iowa was 25th, Illinois 34th, Minnesota 30th, Missouri 32nd and South Dakota 20th. States with the worst SAT scores were Maine, District of Columbia, South Carolina and Hawaii. As far as spending goes, Maine was 5th, District of Columbia 13th, South Carolina 33rd and Hawaii 19th. The state that spent the most per pupil, Vermont, was 30th in SAT scores while the lowest spending state Utah was ranked 20th in SAT scores. National Center for Education Statistics, US Department of Education, 2009.

The United States spending on education as a percentage of its gross domestic product ranks 37th in the world. We are not the best educated people in the world anymore. United Nations, *Human Development Programme*, 2000-2002. In 2006, our country ranked 27th in Math and 22nd in Science. *OECD's Education at a Glance, 2009.*

Can we reach a balance to insure improved test scores to better compete in the world economy while still having time to teach our children literature, foreign language and the arts? With the brainpower in our country, I would think that appropriate solutions can be found by the educational experts. But, please hurry. Time is passing our students by.

16. Socialism

A theory or policy of social organisation (sic) which aims at or advocates the ownership and control of the means of production, capital, land, property, etc, by the community as a whole, and their administration or distribution in the interests of all people. A state of society in which things are held or used in common. Socialism as defined *in The Oxford English Dictionary.*

The word makes people shutter. Being labeled a "Socialist" is about as bad as it gets. Most people don't even know they are voluntary participants in socialistic programs every day. In fact, almost every President has supported programs or helped fund programs which society would deem socialism. That doesn't mean the Presidents were/are socialists. It just means that our society has deemed that not all socialistic programs are bad.

One key element of a socialistic program is the redistribution of wealth, more so from higher income people to lower income people. Look at the definition noted above. How many socialistic programs which have been part of our country's fabric for years come to mind?

How about Social Security retirement benefits? Let's see. The government took part of my taxes and redistributed it to… my Mother. That certainly qualifies as a socialistic program. How about Medicare, Medicaid, farm subsidies, welfare, social security disability, grants to college students, rent subsidies, veteran benefits, federal employee pensions and benefits? Sounds socialistic to me.

Now, some people think President Obama is a socialist because of his healthcare program. Interestingly, on September 20, 2010, *CNBC* issued results of a poll which asked what area of the economy Obama's policies most benefited. The results were "Big banks" and "Wall Street". This is hardly what you would expect from a socialist.

President Reagan signed legislation which resulted in the largest increase in Medicare funding in history. My guess is that very few people, if any, would have considered him a socialist. President George W Bush added thousands of new federal subsidy programs during his two terms in the White House to special interest groups including state governments, businesses, non-profits and individuals. Again, I don't recall anyone calling him a socialist.

To add further to this, take note. There are members in Congress, both in the House and the Senate who are some of the biggest so called "anti-socialists" who have collected farm subsidies for years. Rep. Michelle Bachman and Senator Grassley to name two. This should not surprise anyone. (See my essay on Hypocrisy!)

Now, for those of you who speak to the evils of all socialistic programs as being the devil's work, I have a suggestion. When you reach the appropriate age, tell the government that you are refusing to accept social security and medicare as being part of the socialistic agenda which is going to destroy our country. Also, in fairness, I think you should return all governmental benefits that you have received to date. No? I didn't think so.

__Acknowledgement__

I would like to thank my great friend and cousin David Koester for editing these essays. His comments and insights were very helpful to this writer. God knows I needed it.